Bags of AMERICAN FOLK for violin

Arranged and written by Mary Cohen

© 2010 by Faber Music Ltd
This edition first published in 2010
Bloomsbury House 74-77 Great Russell Street London WC1B 3DA
Music processed by Jeanne Roberts
Cover designed by Lydia Merrills-Ashcroft
Illustration by Andy Cooke
Printed in England by Caligraving Ltd
All rights reserved

ISBN10: 0-571-53416-3
EAN13: 978-0-571-53416-6

To buy Faber Music publications or to find out about the full range of titles available
please contact your local music retailer or Faber Music sales enquiries:

Faber Music Ltd, Burnt Mill, Elizabeth Way, Harlow CM20 2HX
Tel: +44 (0) 1279 82 89 82   Fax: +44 (0) 1279 82 89 83
sales@fabermusic.com   fabermusic.com

Foreword

Bags of American Folk is an introduction to the wonderful world of traditional music – favourite tunes passed down from one generation to the next, many from the early pioneer days. This collection has been carefully selected to include music of many different styles and moods, and it is great to play without needing any accompaniment, although you might like to form a fiddle band with your friends.

Folk music is always changing and developing, and there are lots of ways to personalise tunes once you have mastered the notes. For instance, you can add slides and grace notes, and your own special dynamics. Learn some of these melodies by heart and you will always have something to play for friends and family!

Contents

† These pieces are compatible with *Bags of American Folk for Viola* only. Everything else can be played together with *Bags of American Folk for Viola* and *Bags of American Folk for Cello*.
†† This piece is not compatible with the viola and cello books.

Down in Demerara

Moochin' about

Li'l Liza Jane

Happily

The old grey goose

Spreading the news!

© 2010 by Faber Music Ltd

Little red wagon

Rolling along

Charlie's sweet

With singing tone

The streets of Laredo

Sad and thoughtful

Four in a boat

Lively

She'll be coming round the mountain

Cheerfully

Yankee Doodle

Bright and dandy!

I had a cat

Happily

Old woman

Teasing

Rocky Mountain

Pleading!

Simple gifts

Joyfully

Dixie

Enthusiastically

Boatmen dance, boatmen sing

Nobody knows

Jubilee

My Grandfather's clock

Henry Clay Work

Telling a great story!

O when the saints

Fervently

Jeannie with the light brown hair

Stephen Foster

Heartfelt

Clementine

With strong feeling

On top of Old Smokey

Lazily

I'se the b'y that builds the boat

Brightly

The Yellow Rose of Texas

With determination

Who did?

Energetically

O Susanna

Stephen Foster

Whimsically

Red River Valley

With singing tone

Steal away

Steadily, and with feeling

The shanty boys in the pine

Proud and bold!

Home on the range

John Brown's body

La Cucaracha

Very lively and energetic

She's like the swallow

Sadly

Swing low sweet chariot

With steady movement

Arkensas traveller

Just fast enough . . .

Colonel Sandford C. Faulkner

Shenandoah

Smoothly flowing

Mexican hat dance

Very rhythmic

Casey Jones

Steaming along!

Puttin' on the blue check shirt

Mary Cohen

Havin' a good time!